This
Loretta story
belongs to

....

To my gorgeous daughters,
my forever source of inspiration,
the reason I write.

First published in Great Britain 2022

Text and illustrations copyright © Barbara Gianquitto 2022

Author: Barbara Gianquitto
Illustrator: Sarah Parkinson
Editor: Stefanie Briar

The moral rights of the author have been asserted

All rights reserved

No part of this publication may be reproduced or transmitted by any means, electronic, mechanical, photocopying, or otherwise, without the prior permission of the author

ISBN: 978-1-7395880-2-1

Loretta
and the Monday Morning Blues

By Barbara Gianquitto

Illustrated by Sarah Parkinson

It was a cold Monday morning; the clock was **ticking fast,** and it was time to start a new week in Loretta's house.

Mum was rushing in the house as usual, it was already late, and Mondays were always very busy!

"It is time to go to school, Loretta!

Wake up!"

Not a lot of light was filtering through the grey sky that morning, and Loretta was hiding under the covers crying.

"Oh, Loretta. Why don't you want to go to school, darling?"

"I just don't want to, mamma" said Loretta with big tears coming down her face.

"Okay Loretta, come out and
at least give me a hug,
it will make you feel better"
said mum in a calming voice.

She knew that Loretta was always happy
once she got to school

she had lots of friends,
and there was nothing wrong there.

"I don't want to get out of bed, mamma."

She knew they were late for school, but that morning, instead of rushing,

mum slowed down and said:

"Everything is okay, you are okay"

"But I don't **feel** it," cried Loretta.

"Of course it is.

Sometimes we are happy.

Other times we feel sad.

Adults feel like this as well you know?

That doesn't mean you are not okay."

"You see Loretta,
 all day long, we have so many thoughts going through our heads.

They **come** and **go**.

Sadness is one of them.
   But we don't come and go with them.

   I promise you,
      this thought won't stay with you all day."

Loretta slowly got up and got dressed into her school uniform.

The room was quiet, and Loretta was still sad.

Then suddenly, Mum said quite loudly:

"Oh, wait! Where is it?"

"What, mamma?"
Loretta immediately asked.

"Hmmm, I had it right here,
maybe it's under the covers!" said Mum.

"Quick, help me look for it!"

But there was **nothing there.**

"Maybe it's in one of your wardrobe drawers!

Come, let's look!"
hurried Mum.

"Mamma, there are just **socks** in this drawer"
said Loretta, puzzled.

"Hmmm, I bet it's in the desk's drawer!"
said mum

Loretta quickly rushed to open the drawers, but she only found **pens** and **paper**.

They kept going **all around the room.**

They looked in the toy box

under the rug

in **every** drawer

under the **desk**

even in
the bin!

Still not knowing what they were looking for, Loretta lifted **the pillow.**

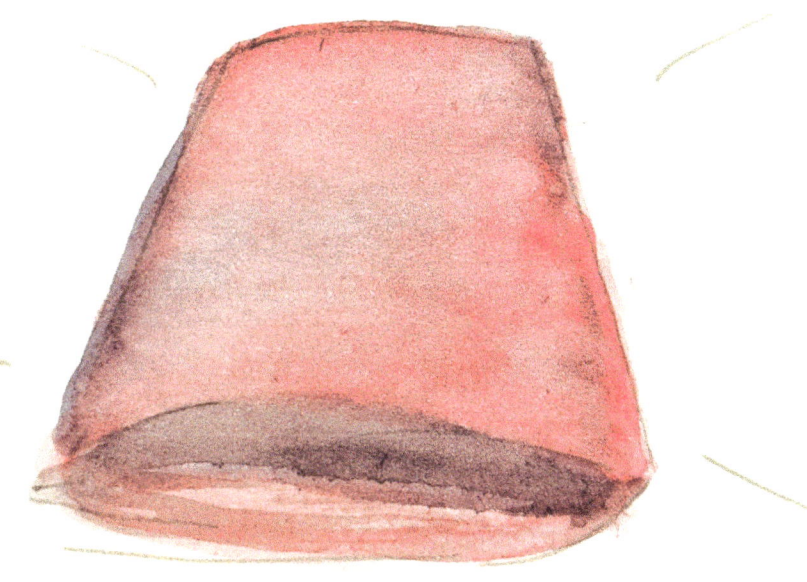

Loretta couldn't see **anything**

so she looked at Mum with disappointment.

But mum started to laugh and said:

"Oh, there it is, I found it, I found it!"

and she picked it up from under the pillow,
cupping her hands to keep it safe.

Mum moved closer to Loretta and slowly opened her hands.

Loretta's eyes **widened**

Mum's hands were

empty...

"Ah Loretta, not everything that is *precious* can easily be seen.

Look closely..."

"There is your smile!

That's what I was looking for!

Happiness sometimes hides
in the most
unexpected
places!"

And like this,

Loretta's frown melted away.

"You see little one,

    some days we wake up with a smile.

And some days we wake up with a frown.

And that is okay."

And on days when you don't feel like smiling,
remember that it is **just a thought.**

Like a cloud passing by,
sadness is not there to stay long.

And when you feel really sad,
remember the day when you and mamma
looked for your smile everywhere...

and found it **under your pillow!**"

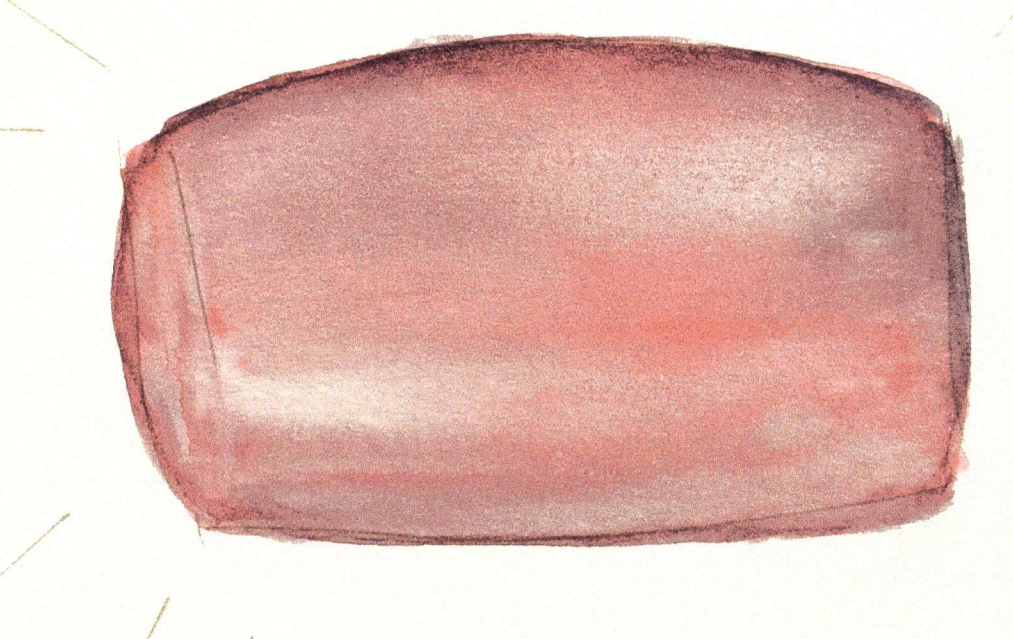

Barbara Gianquitto
Author

Barbara Gianquitto is a poet and writer, best known as the author of the best selling poetry collections '4:04am Thoughts' and 'Awakening of the Heart'.

She is also a mum of 2, and her mission is to reach a younger audience to convey the importance of validating children's feelings to better equip them for the future.

Her soft, open and unique voice has gathered the interest of over 30 thousand readers on social media across the world and BBC national radio.

As a graduate in communication and psychology, Barbara has a passion for the power of words, inspiring her readers to dive deeper into their own power and self-discovery. Born and raised in Italy, Barbara currently lives in the United Kingdom with her family and two grumpy cats.

She drinks far too much coffee, follows the Moon and all its phases and is a hopeless romantic.

"Words are all we have in this world, we should use them more often."

Barbara's poetry '4:04am Thoughts' and 'Awakening of the Heart'

Sarah Parkinson
Illustrator

Sarah has been writing and illustrating childrens books ever since she was inspired walking through a local park with her newborn daughter. Her bestselling series 'The Tales of Willow Park' is influenced by exciting facts in nature that can spark children's curiosity in their world around them.

In an effort to inspire more children to draw, Sarah delivers drawing workshops online and in schools and loves every minute of it. She writes and paints her stories at home with her daughter and husband in Oswestry, Shropshire.

You can find more about Barbara's work and upcoming projects at www.barbaragianquitto.com.

 @barbara.gianquitto.author

 @BarbaraNgianquitto

 @bgianquitto

@barbara.gianquitto

 @sparkauthor

 @sparkyauthor

 @sparkyauthor

 @SparkyAuthor

www.ingramcontent.com/pod-product-compliance
Lightning Source LLC
Chambersburg PA
CBHW051321110526
44590CB00031B/4428